FRANKLIN PIERCE

The Presidents of the United States

George Washington
1789–1797

John Adams
1797–1801

Thomas Jefferson
1801–1809

James Madison
1809–1817

James Monroe
1817–1825

John Quincy Adams
1825–1829

Andrew Jackson
1829–1837

Martin Van Buren
1837–1841

William Henry Harrison
1841

John Tyler
1841–1845

James Polk
1845–1849

Zachary Taylor
1849–1850

Millard Fillmore
1850–1853

Franklin Pierce
1853–1857

James Buchanan
1857–1861

Abraham Lincoln
1861–1865

Andrew Johnson
1865–1869

Ulysses S. Grant
1869–1877

Rutherford B. Hayes
1877–1881

James Garfield
1881

Chester Arthur
1881–1885

Grover Cleveland
1885–1889

Benjamin Harrison
1889–1893

Grover Cleveland
1893–1897

William McKinley
1897–1901

Theodore Roosevelt
1901–1909

William H. Taft
1909–1913

Woodrow Wilson
1913–1921

Warren Harding
1921–1923

Calvin Coolidge
1923–1929

Herbert Hoover
1929–1933

Franklin D. Roosevelt
1933–1945

Harry Truman
1945–1953

Dwight Eisenhower
1953–1961

John F. Kennedy
1961–1963

Lyndon B. Johnson
1963–1969

Richard Nixon
1969–1974

Gerald Ford
1974–1977

Jimmy Carter
1977–1981

Ronald Reagan
1981–1989

George H. W. Bush
1989–1993

William J. Clinton
1993–2001

George W. Bush
2001–2009

Barack Obama
2009–

FRANKLIN PIERCE

DAVID C. KING

mc Marshall Cavendish
Benchmark
New York

Marshall Cavendish Benchmark
99 White Plains Road
Tarrytown, NY 10591-5502
www.marshallcavendish.us

All Internet addresses were correct at the time of printing.

Library of Congress Cataloging-in-Publication Data

King, David C.
Franklin Pierce / by David C. King.
p. cm. — (Presidents and their times)
Summary: "Provides comprehensive information on President Franklin Pierce and places him
within his historical and cultural context. Also explored are the formative events of his times
and how he responded"—Provided by publisher.
Includes bibliographical references and index.
ISBN 978-0-7614-3624-9
1. Pierce, Franklin, 1804–1869—Juvenile literature. 2. Presidents—United States—
Biography—Juvenile literature. I. Title.
E432.K56 2009
973.6'6092—dc22
[B]
2008016003

Editor: Christine Florie
Publisher: Michelle Bisson
Art Director: Anahid Hamparian
Series Designer: Alex Ferrari

Photo research by Connie Gardner

Cover photo by The Granger collection

The photographs in this book are used by permission and through the courtesy of:*Bridgeman Art Library:*
Healy, George Peter Alexander (1808–94) Private Collection, 3, 97, 99 (R); *Corbis:* Bettmann, 8, 13, 20,
41 (B), 48; David and Janice L. Frent, 50; Gianni Dagli Orti, 59; *Alamy:* Visual Arts Library, 51; *Getty
Images:* Hulton Archive, 11, 16, 36, 38, 86; George Henry Durrie, Bridgeman Art Library, 14; William
Aiken Walker, 30; American School, The Bridgeman Art Library, 40 (B); Matthew Brady, Bridgeman
Art Library, 88; *North Wind Picture Archive:* 28, 34, 57; *The Granger Collection:* 19, 22, 25, 26, 32, 40
(T), 46, 55, 61, 63, 68, 70, 76, 78, 81, 92, 98 (R and L); *Art Resource:* National Portrait Gallery,
Smithsonian Institution, 94, 99 (L).

Printed in Malaysia
1 3 5 6 4 2

CONTENTS

★ ★ ★ ★ ★ ★ ★ ★ ★ ★ ★ ★ ★ ★ ★ ★

FRANKLIN PIERCE

Many historians see Franklin Pierce as an "undistinguished" president, whose administration lacked the strength to lead the nation during its dispute over slavery.

$\mathcal{F}$ranklin Pierce is one of America's forgotten presidents. If people today remember him at all, it is as one of several undistinguished presidents whose terms clustered around those of the two giants of the mid-1800s—Andrew Jackson (1829–1837) and Abraham Lincoln (1861–1865). Pierce was rejected in his lifetime—even his own Democratic Party failed to nominate him for a second term. History has not been kind to him, either. In a 1962 poll of historians he was ranked twenty-eighth out of thirty-one presidents; a *U.S. News & World Report* survey in 2007 placed him ahead of only James Buchanan, Warren G. Harding, and Andrew Johnson.

When Pierce was elected in 1852, however, his future was full of promise. He was a handsome, intelligent, popular, and persuasive speaker who had never lost an election, and he was young—the youngest man elected to the presidency until Theodore Roosevelt, in 1904. Peter Wallner, author of two Pierce biographies, writes that this president was "one of the most charming, charismatic, and interesting men to ever hold the nation's highest office." His close friend, the great writer Nathaniel Hawthorne, described him as "deep, deep, deep, [with] most of the chief elements of a great ruler."

CHILDHOOD AND EDUCATION

Franklin Pierce was born on November 23, 1804, in a log cabin on a branch of New Hampshire's Contoocook River, outside the village of Hillsborough. At the time of his birth, central New Hampshire was still part of New England's frontier, a hilly land with short summers and long, snow-filled winters.

His father, General Benjamin Pierce, was the leading figure of this frontier community. He had been a Revolutionary War hero, a man with little education and few cultural refinements—rough and domineering but, at the same time, compassionate and kind. Soon after Franklin was born, the general moved his family into a large, stately home in Hillsborough's Lower Village.

Franklin was one of nine children. He had five brothers and three sisters, the last born in 1812. He was said to be "robust, active, and devilish"—a boy who was quick with his fists or with a practical joke. The boy was very fond of his mother, Anna Kendrick Pierce (1768–1838). "She was a most affectionate and tender mother," he wrote, "strong in many points and weak in others, but always weak on the side of kindness and deep affection." Unfortunately, he seemed to have inherited one of his mother's weaknesses—a dependence on alcohol.

Throughout his life Franklin was strongly influenced by his father. Over and over he listened to the story of how the young Benjamin was plowing a field in 1775 when word came that patriot militiamen were trading gunshots with British redcoats on Lexington Green in Massachusetts—the opening shots of the American Revolution. Benjamin grabbed his father's shotgun, headed for the road leading from Lexington to Boston, and never looked back.

There were countless Revolutionary War stories for Pierce to listen to. His father joined General George Washington's Continental Army after fighting in the Battle of Bunker Hill.

Pierce's father, General Benjamin Pierce, was an American soldier and politician.

He rose steadily in rank while fighting in New York at Fort Ticonderoga and Saratoga. With Washington, he suffered through a winter at Valley Forge. For the remainder of the war he was stationed at the United States Military Academy at West Point along the Hudson River, finally taking possession of New York with Washington. Benjamin left the army in 1784 with the rank of general.

General Pierce remained a leader of frontier New Hampshire. During a public life that stretched over fifty-seven years, he held a number of minor political positions until he was elected governor of New Hampshire in 1827 and again in 1829.

To solidify his position, the general had his house built on a main post road so that he received a constant flow of traveling government officials and visitors. He also followed the common practice of obtaining a license to sell alcohol, which transformed the Pierce sitting room into an informal tavern.

This often-crowded "tavern" provided an important part of young Franklin's education. During the War of 1812, for example, scores of militiamen and volunteers traveled the post road to and from the battlefronts. Many stopped at the Pierce tavern, and Franklin listened eagerly to their stories of the war as Anna and older daughters Elizabeth and Nancy scurried to serve the guests. In addition, two of his brothers and a brother-in-law had served in the army, the latter being celebrated as a great hero of land battles in Canada. Their stories, and those of his father, filled the boy's head with dreams of military glory. For years to come he would long for his chance to display battlefield courage and leadership. He was to have his chance when the United States went to war against Mexico in 1846.

Pierce's father transformed the family home's sitting room into a tavern where travelers could stop and share news and stories.

EDUCATION

Young Franklin learned to read and write at a little brick school-house in Hillsborough. He was considered very bright and a fast learner, but he also slipped away often to wander through the woods or take a dip in one of the rushing streams near the village. In 1818 he enrolled at Hancock Academy in Hancock,

THE UNIQUE CULTURE OF NEW ENGLAND

New England in the early nineteenth century was a land of villages and small farms. In the larger villages, stately houses lined streets shaded by graceful elms and maples. Craft shops, inns, and steepled churches were clustered around village greens, where sheep and cattle grazed and the local militia drilled.

In many ways it seemed like a slow-paced life, but New England was actually bursting with energy. Most of the people were hardworking farmers who used remarkable ingenuity to force a modest prosperity out of the stubborn, rocky soil. The majority of these "Yankee" farm families took an active interest in political affairs. Through town meetings, they participated in a form of democracy that continues to be a model studied by students of government.

This New England setting also produced some of America's greatest writers, poets, and philosophers, including Ralph Waldo Emerson, Henry David Thoreau, Herman Melville, and Walt Whitman. Two other greats—novelist Nathaniel Hawthorne and poet Henry Wadsworth Longfellow—were college mates of Pierce's at the tiny Bowdoin College, in Maine.

New Hampshire, and in 1820, he finished his college preparation at Francestown Academy in Francestown, New Hampshire, demonstrating skill in Latin composition and Greek translation, as well as a knowledge of geography and math.

That same year Pierce entered Bowdoin College. He made friends easily and enjoyed college life more for its social and recreational possibilities than for book work. In fact, by the end of his sophomore year, he had drifted to the bottom of his class.

Seeing his ranking was a shock for Pierce, and he became determined to reverse his standing. By commencement day in 1824, he had achieved success in languages, math, philosophy,

In 1820 Franklin Pierce entered Bowdoin College in Brunswick, Maine.

and history and had done well enough in chemistry and mineralogy to graduate fourth in his class.

During his college years, Pierce's perspective on religion began changing. Although his mother had always been devout, he had paid little attention to her beliefs. Halfway through his college career, however, he shared a room with a Methodist student named Zenas Caldwell. Caldwell's devotion to college and to his religion impressed Pierce. He began attending church with his roommate. "He conquered me by his faith and by his Christian life," Pierce wrote. While he deeply admired Caldwell's strong faith, Pierce did not share it. It would be years before he reached a point where his membership in a church became important to him. However, his core belief in religious tolerance was one principle Pierce would follow throughout his lifetime—even when it made him unpopular with the voters.

LAW, POLITICS, AND MARRIAGE

After graduating from Bowdoin in 1824, Pierce returned to the family home in Hillsborough to begin studying law. He was surprised to find that the family home had elegant new furnishings, including scenic wallpaper, the last word in extravagant home decor.

Pierce's father had decided to enter politics with the goal of eventually running for governor. The newly decorated house provided a perfect meeting place, with its comfortable innlike rooms and its location on the busy highway to Concord, the state capital. In an age when there was no television or radio and only a few newspapers, the best way for a potential candidate to become well known to voters was through public meetings and face-to-face contact.

While he observed his father's meetings with the constant round of political visitors, young Pierce began his own study of the law. There were few formal law schools in the early 1800s, so he followed the usual practice of "reading the law" with a well-known local lawyer. Pierce studied with Judge Levi Woodbury in Portsmouth, New Hampshire, for a year, then for one year at Northampton Law School, followed by a year of study with Judge William Parker in Amherst, New Hampshire.

Pierce was admitted to the New Hampshire Bar in 1827. He arrived back home in time to join the family's celebration of Benjamin's election as governor of New Hampshire that year. It was

Franklin Pierce returned to the family home in Hillsborough, New Hampshire, upon his graduation from Bowdoin College in 1824.

a great honor for the old Revolutionary War hero, and the entire family joined in the carriage procession to Concord, where he would serve a one-year term.

PIERCE'S LAW CAREER

To help Pierce launch his law career, his father built him an office across the road from the family house. He also helped his son buy a deceased lawyer's law library of seventy-five volumes.

Pierce's law practice, opened in 1827, did not start out well. In fact, he suffered humiliating defeats in his first two cases.

The Age of Jackson

Andrew Jackson was elected president of the United States in 1828. His two terms in office brought a new spirit of democracy to the nation. The new age began with voting reforms, expanding voting rolls by allowing men without property to vote, and giving many Americans a stronger feeling that they had a say in their government.

Although many reforms took place during Jackson's terms, it was not due to his influence. The Jacksonians strongly believed in the Con-

stitution and followed what it stated as closely as possible. They supported the idea of states' rights but frowned on too much power going to the national government. Jackson's opinions on governmental control had been demonstrated earlier, when he helped to destroy the Bank of the United States. He did so out of a growing concern that it would exert too much control over people and individual state banks.

Jackson felt that the major issues of his presidency—temperance, or drinking alcohol in moderation, immigration, and outlawing slavery—should not be decided by the government, because that course of action risked taking away the rights of the common man.

Both Franklin Pierce and his father agreed with Jackson's ideals. They and other Jackson Democrats, as they were called, adamantly stood for the idea that the less government involved itself, the better chance everyone had of keeping their freedom, making their own decisions, and pursuing their interests without governmental interference.

His friend Nathaniel Hawthorne noted that rather than depressing him, the defeats actually brought out his "innate self-confidence."

As he developed his skills in the courtroom, Pierce began winning case after case. He took on every kind that came his way—criminal or civil. He argued disputes over wills, damages, property lines, contracts, murders, slander, and libel.

The legal profession in the nineteenth century was rooted more in the power of personality and speech than on knowledge of the law. Juries were made up of local citizens—men who had little schooling, if any. They tended to doze off or gaze out the window unless aroused by the fiery words of an articulate lawyer. One of Pierce's biographers wrote that lawyers "made themselves practiced in oratory [so] that they might sway human emotions by the voice and personality. Flowery, fiery,

Though Franklin Pierce's law practice began with a slow start, he developed into a respected attorney.

rhetorical, flowing, flamboyant, their speech drew a pleasure-starved people out of themselves, stimulated their imaginations and roused their feelings."

Pierce worked hard to develop his courtroom skills. He built on what Hawthorne called "his native habit of close and careful observation," developing "a vastly greater power than [before] over the minds with which he came in contact."

Pierce researched his cases thoroughly and, during trials, constantly studied the faces of the jurors, searching for clues about how his arguments were being received. He was a long and lean 5 feet 10 inches tall, making him a commanding presence in the courtroom. His handsome appearance and persuasive speaking style added to the impression he created, leading one news reporter to write, "Frank Pierce is the most popular man of his age that I know of in New Hampshire." After he had been practicing law for several years, the Chief Justice of New Hampshire said, "The eloquence of Mr. Pierce is of a character not easily forgotten. He understands men, their passions and their feelings."

STATE POLITICAL LEADER

Pierce had long been intrigued by the world of politics. He had grown up in a household where political discussions were daily fare. Of all his personal assets, probably none was greater than his ability to get along with people. He had great personal charm, made friends easily, and seemed never to forget a name or a face.

In 1829 the town of Hillsborough showed its confidence in him by electing him as its representative in the New Hampshire Legislature (or General Court). He was twenty-four years old. At the same time, his father Benjamin, who had lost a bid for reelection for governor in 1828, managed to win his second term. In 1830 father and son headed to Concord as both the oldest and the youngest members of the state government at the time.

Pierce found that his skill in persuasion served him well in the state legislature. He quickly rose to leadership positions and was easily reelected to three more terms. During his last two terms Pierce also served as speaker of the 229-seat legislature. At only twenty-six years old, he was the New Hampshire Legislature's youngest speaker. He used this post to begin organizing the state's Democratic Party.

Pierce's name was not associated with any special legislation in the General Court sessions. Instead, his true genius was in his organization skills. In his last two terms as speaker he knew how to use the considerable power of the office.

Through persuasion, trade-offs, and deals, Pierce built a strong party. Under his leadership the state party organized public support on particular issues or behind certain candidates. Biographer Roy Nichols wrote, "The Democratic party was to become for Pierce his family, his fraternity, his church, and his country."

During the 1830s Pierce became increasingly well known and popular throughout the state. He received accolades when he was appointed an aide to the governor at that time—an honorary position, but one that allowed him to be addressed as "Colonel" Pierce. This added to his stature, but Pierce was aware that it was not a good substitute for actual military experience. He was keenly aware that his father's fame as a hero of the Revolution had practically guaranteed his success in politics. Pierce could not imagine how he could ever gain that kind of experience.

In 1833 he was elected to the U.S. Congress. There was no real campaigning necessary for election to the House of Representatives when Pierce's name was put forward. His popularity as the party leader in New Hampshire gave him an easy victory. At that time he took office as the youngest member of the House of

Pierce's youth and good looks were tempered by dedication to his work and genuine sincerity.

Representatives. His life was changing in another dramatic way, too, as he prepared to marry Jane Appleton.

An Unusual Partnership

Pierce had met Jane Means Appleton in 1828. Jane was the daughter of the Reverend Jesse Appleton, minister of the Congregational Church in Hampton, New Hampshire. During most of her childhood and teenage years, her father was also president of Bowdoin College. When the Reverend Appleton died suddenly in 1819, his widow moved the family to Amherst. Franklin Pierce entered the school a few months later.

Franklin Pierce married Jane Means Appleton in 1834.

Soon after they met in Amherst, Jane and Franklin fell in love. From the beginning friends and family thought they were strangely mismatched. Jane was very shy, not at all social, and quite frail. She was often ill, possibly due to tuberculosis. It left her weak and nervous. Pierce was almost exactly the opposite. He was lively, sociable, loved meeting people, and, as biographer Roy Nichols said, he was equally "at home in political [meeting] and tavern."

The two families were not enthusiastic about the match. Jane's mother was part of Amherst's "aristocracy," a group who were still considered believers in old Federalist politics; they wanted the national government to support the New England merchant class. By contrast, Pierce was a Democrat from a rough frontier area, a believer in more democratic policies.

Despite these differences, Jane stood up to her family, and the two married on November 19, 1834, a few days before Franklin's thirtieth birthday. The newlyweds planned to honeymoon on their way to Washington, D.C., and to set up housekeeping in Hillsborough after the term. In time, the Appletons came to love and respect Pierce for his dedication to Jane.

REPRESENTING NEW HAMPSHIRE

Three

*T*he nation was growing and changing with remarkable speed in the 1830s and 1840s. For example, news which had once taken days or weeks to travel only a few hundred miles, was now received in minutes thanks to the telegraph. Other new inventions, such as the steamboat and steam railroad, were revolutionizing travel. In spite of such advances, there were many reminders that society was in a state of transition. Consider the Pierces' first trip to Washington. First they traveled to Boston and from there rode a stagecoach to a port on Long Island Sound. A boat took them across to New York City, where they caught another steamboat to Amboy, New Jersey. A steam-powered train, racing at a speed of 18 miles per hour, carried them from Amboy to Bordentown. After a steamboat journey to Philadelphia, another boat took

This 1837 poster advertises for "speedy" rail and canal travel.

them to New Castle, Delaware, where another railroad journey of 16 miles carried them to Frenchtown. One more steamboat took the couple to Baltimore, and finally a rough 40-mile stagecoach ride of seven hours deposited them in Washington.

The nation's capital was also in transition, including a few reconstruction projects dating back to 1813, when the British burned much of the city. The unfinished dome of the Capitol still looked so ugly that people called it the "iron pot." The broad avenues of the city were unpaved and turned to dust in dry weather and into muddy quagmires in the rain. The wide expanses made the houses look small and out of place.

The Pierces lived in a ten dollar-per-week rooming house. They paid an extra $1.50 for the added comfort of a rocking chair. Mrs. Pierce put up a brave front for her husband's sake, but her dislike of politicians was reinforced by encounters with rough-hewn congressmen from frontier districts. Her upper-class sensibilities were offended by their hard drinking and crude manners, including frequent spitting and keeping their hats on indoors.

Political Issues

Pierce served two terms in the House of Representatives, easily winning reelection in 1835. His career as a congressman received a boost when his friend, James K. Polk, was chosen for the powerful position of Speaker of the House. Polk was able to assign Pierce to several select committees, including a nine-man committee charged with proposing a statement on Congress's position regarding slavery.

Slavery, in fact, became a troublesome issue in the mid-1830s for the first time in more than a decade. In 1820 the so-called **Missouri Compromise** allowed Maine to enter the Union as a free state (in which slavery was outlawed) and Missouri as a slave state. The compromise meant that the Union would continue to have equal numbers of slave states and free states—and therefore equal numbers of senators from each. In addition, slavery was to be prohibited in the territories north of Missouri.

Congressman Pierce was torn about the issue of slavery. On the one hand, he disliked the idea of it, saying, "I consider slavery

In the mid-1830s the issue of slavery was a hot political topic of the day.

a social and political evil, and most sincerely wish that it has no existence upon the face of the earth." On the other hand, the practice was also quite constitutional, and Pierce was a firm believer in what the Founding Fathers had set forth. George Washington, Thomas Jefferson, John Adams, Benjamin Franklin, and James Madison had established that the legality of slavery was an issue that should be left up to the individual states to decide, and Pierce agreed.

In a letter to John P. Hale, a friend and classmate at Bowdoin, in December 1835, Pierce wrote, "One thing must be perfectly apparent to every intelligent man. This **abolition** movement must be crushed or there is an end to the Union." Pierce recognized that the issue of slavery had the potential to tear the nation apart through a civil war. He was right—and a few decades later, his prediction would come true as the North and the South went to war against each other.

In one of Pierce's speeches he insisted that the people of the South had a constitutional right to own slaves. He viewed those who favored the abolition of slavery as a tiny group of misguided agitators who threatened the safety of the Union. The nine-member committee charged with preparing a statement regarding slavery issued a detailed document concluding that Congress had no authority to interfere with slavery either in the states or in the District of Columbia.

The issue was made more complicated in May 1836 with the news that Texas had won its independence from Mexico. The complicating factor was that Texas allowed slavery, and antislavery forces in Congress were insistent that the admission of another slave state would not be tolerated. Now that the slavery

Reform and Abolitionism

Beginning with the presidency of Andrew Jackson, a wave of reform swept the country. The Age of Jackson had brought greater democracy in American political life, while growth, new inventions, and economic prosperity had made people feel that progress could continue indefinitely.

In this atmosphere many began to feel that progress could be made in all aspects of American life. In religion, camp meetings and revivals were held across the country as people experienced a great moral and spiritual awakening.

A number of nonreligious groups tried to create perfect societies called utopias. Fruitlands and Brook Farm in Massachusetts, as well as others, did not last long, but a few, such as the Oneida Community in New York, survived until the early twenty-first century. Ideas of reform

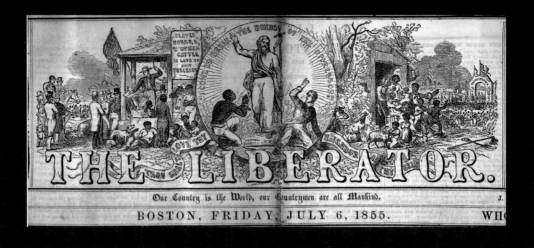

also led to a great push for free public education, at least for white children living in the North. Others sought progress by forming societies that fought for temperance.

Abolitionism—the movement to end slavery—also grew in these years. Antislavery organizations were formed, and the first abolitionist newspapers appeared, including William Lloyd Garrison's *The Liberator* (left). Many women's rights advocates joined the drive to end slavery.

issue was being debated openly again, it could not be suppressed. In fact, the dark cloud of disunion and the possibility of civil war now hung over the nation and would remain there until the storm finally broke, twenty-five years later.

For Franklin Pierce ambivalence toward the slavery issue—and his determination to preserve the Union at all costs—would remain with him for the rest of his life and would be the major factor in determining the success or failure of his political career.

While Pierce remained consistent on the slavery issue throughout his life, he displayed flexibility on other subjects. During his time in the House of Representatives, for example, he wanted Congress to withhold funding for the United States Military Academy at West Point. The academy, located on the Hudson River in New York State, was the major educational institution for training the future officers of the U.S. Army. Pierce had become convinced that many cadets were there simply to receive a free education and had no intention of serving their country after graduation. Congress voted to provide the funds, in spite of Pierce's opposition.

After his own experiences with West Point-trained officers in the Mexican War in 1846, however, Pierce openly admitted that he had been wrong and that West Point provided an outstanding service for the country. From that time on he was an avid supporter of the academy.

Initially, Franklin Pierce was not supportive of governmental funding for the United States Military Academy at West Point. That view changed after his own military experiences during the Mexican War.

Personal Trials

Living in the nation's capital for one session of Congress proved to be more than enough for Mrs. Pierce. She decided not to return with her husband for the next session. Although Pierce missed his wife and tried to write to her every day, he thought he would enjoy his time with other congressmen who had left their wives at home. He was wrong.

His greatest difficulty was his frequent bouts of drinking. He would often drink with his congressional friends, especially since his wife was not there to watch over his behavior and make sure he did not return to his old habits. One night Pierce and his friend Clement March spent the evening visiting the theater and several taverns. March described the night as "the greatest frolic of my life." He also went on to list the evening's drinking menu, including large quantities of brandy, champagne, and wine.

Everything came to a climax in late February 1836. Pierce went to the theater with Henry Wise and Edward Hannegan. All three men had been drinking for some time before they arrived. Soon after, Hannegan got into an argument with an acquaintance. The dispute grew louder and more heated until finally, Hannegan drew a gun. The weapon was taken away before anyone could be injured. Pierce was so upset by the embarrassment of the situation that he became physically ill. This humiliating incident was enough to inspire him to eventually quit drinking altogether.

Soon after, Pierce's ragged nerves were jarred by yet another incident. He was elated by the news that he and Jane's first child, Franklin Jr., had been born, but the joy was cut short by another message received three days later that the infant had died.

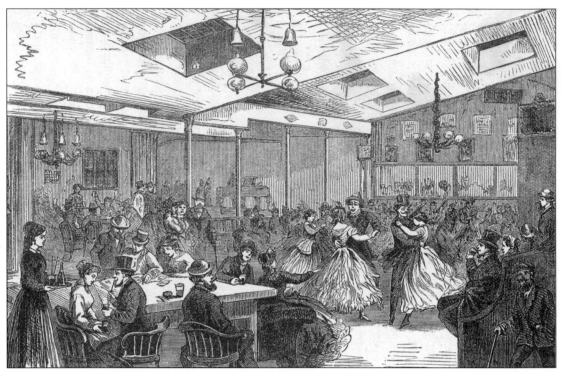

During his time in Congress, Pierce would visit the taverns of Washington, D.C.

Pierce's time serving in the House of Representatives was over, and it had not been easy. He had not introduced any important bills, nor had he given any memorable speeches. He worked hard on various committees, however, and he remained a steady supporter of President Jackson, especially when the president was being attacked by his enemies. Years later the former president Jackson spoke to a friend about Pierce's talents and his patriotism, saying, "The interests of the country would be safe in such hands."

THE YOUNGEST SENATOR

When Pierce's term in the House of Representatives ended in 1837, he looked forward to spending time developing his law practice. Jane, of course, was delighted to have him away from Washington. In addition, they both hoped to move from Hillsborough to Concord; she thought the people of Concord would be more to her liking, and he hoped the move would expand his law practice.

Before Pierce could focus on his legal profession, however, another opportunity arose. In May 1836 Senator Isaac Hill from New Hampshire resigned from the Senate. This left a gap, and many people thought immediately of Pierce as a good choice to finish out Hill's term. There were at least six candidates running for the seat, and each one of them had strong supporters who argued spiritedly for their personal favorite. John Page, a New Hampshire lawyer and political figure, was chosen, however. Pierce was elected to the full term following Page's. He began in March 1837.

Jane Pierce did not seem thrilled by her husband's new position, but she was determined to make the best of it. She decided she would again accompany him to Washington.

At age thirty-two Pierce became the youngest senator at that time, proudly holding one of the most important political offices in the nation. The Senate was a much more imposing body

In 1837 Franklin
Pierce became
the nation's
youngest senator
at thirty-two
years old.

than the House of Representatives. There were only fifty-two members, who met in elegant surroundings. The nation's vice president, Richard M. Johnson, presided, sitting beneath a great scarlet canopy, while above him, a sculpted eagle seemed about to soar out over the assemblage.

The Slavery Issue Heats Up

During his time in the Senate (1837–1842) Pierce rarely spoke from the floor. One reason for this was that the chamber was dominated by some of the greatest men in the Senate's history. Three who towered over all others were Henry Clay of Kentucky, John C. Calhoun of South Carolina, and Daniel Webster of Massachusetts. Pierce hoped to learn by observing these great orators.

The young senator worked hard on several committees but soon found himself speaking on the issue of slavery. His own state opened the subject by submitting a petition requesting a **gag rule** in the Senate.

In an eloquent speech from the Senate floor, Pierce argued against the idea of imposing a gag rule. He said he was more than willing to vote against a petition, but that it was important to receive it—all citizens had a right to petition their government. Besides, he said, refusing to receive a petition played into the hands of the abolitionists, who could claim that their rights were being denied. His objection was ignored by his fellow Democrats, and the gag rule was passed.

Before Pierce's term in the Senate, the slavery issue was complicated further when Texas won independence from Mexico. The Texans, governed by Americans, wanted to be **annexed** by the United States, but in 1836 the State of Vermont submitted

The Senate's Three Giants

For about thirty years, up to 1850, the debates in the Senate were frequently dominated by the speeches of Clay, Calhoun, and Webster. All three were staunch defenders of the union of states. Henry Clay (left; 1777–1852) of Kentucky was known as the "Great Compromiser," especially for working out compromises between the slaveholding states of the South and the nonslave states of the North.

Daniel Webster (below; 1782–1852) had been one of the most eloquent orators on behalf of the Union for many years. He was also a close friend of Pierce's. Although Webster was a Whig and Pierce was a Democrat, they had been born in the same state and had spent quite a bit of time together in the past. The two were so often spotted together that Pierce was scolded by a fellow Democrat, who believed that this friendship weakened Pierce's political reputation. In response, Pierce stated, "So long as I feel that the friendship and intimacy of Mr. Webster are more important to me than a seat in the [Congress], as I do feel it, I shall not likely be intimidated by any threats like the one in your note."

In a famous 1830 debate with Senator Robert Hayne of South Carolina, Webster concluded his final speech with the ringing words "Liberty *and* Union, now and forever, one and inseparable!" John C. Calhoun (left; 1782–1850) also defended the Union but, when that defense conflicted with the rights of his state, he insisted that his state must come first.

Their last moment in the spotlight came in 1850, when California applied for statehood as a free state. Admitting California as a free state would upset the North-South balance, and once again there was danger that the Union would dissolve and perhaps plunge into Civil War.

Clay tried to save the Union with a series of agreements that became known as the Compromise of 1850 (or the Great Compromise). Calhoun, ill and close to death, had to have a friend read his speech, which bitterly opposed the plan. Agitation over slavery, he argued, would snap "the cords which bind these states together. . . . Nothing will be left to hold the states together except force." Three days later he was carried into the Senate Chamber to hear Webster deliver a dramatic support of the compromise, which was then passed. This compromise would soon become of great importance to the career of Franklin Pierce.

a petition to the Senate requesting that annexation be denied. Abolitionists were thrilled because Texas would have entered as a slave state. Southerners were furious; it was the first time an entire state had taken such a step.

Calhoun responded with a series of six resolutions, with the central idea that slavery was essentially a matter for the states to deal with. Pierce supported Calhoun's resolutions and delivered a lengthy speech explaining his reasons. He had come to feel that the antislavery agitation was the work of "a few misguided fanatics" who were joined by political schemers bent on destroying the Constitution. Pierce was convinced that fighting this alliance was essential to preserving the Union, and he was pleased that the Senate approved the resolution.

Resigning from the Senate

In 1838 the Pierce family made their move to Concord, where they would live for the rest of their lives. Pierce took on a new law partner, Asa Fowler, and then went back to Washington without his wife. While living alone, he was determined to avoid the pitfalls of socializing and drinking. He established a strict regimen to deal with loneliness, to improve his health, and to address his inability to embrace religion.

That year, a number of family matters required his attention. His mother died in 1838, and his father died a year later. There were also deaths in Jane's family. Also in 1839, a second son, Frank Robert, was born, and then two years later a third son, named Benny.

By 1840 Pierce's enthusiasm for his Senate career was fading. His law practice was demanding his attention—as was his growing family. He felt that he had lost his "usual elasticity of spirits and capability for business." Mrs. Pierce was even more disillusioned. "Oh, how I wish he was out of political life!" she said. "How much better it would be for him on every account!"

Finally, in 1842, he resigned and returned to New Hampshire. He was now a private citizen.

AT LAST, A LAW CAREER

*I*n the spring of 1842 Pierce's life entered a new phase. Since he was no longer a politician, he could focus on being a lawyer. With their boys in tow, the Pierces moved into their new house on Montgomery Street in Concord and looked forward to a more stable home life and a steadier and stronger income.

Since he first held public office in 1833, Pierce had had little time to devote to his law practice. He now went back to it eagerly, establishing his office near his home and the courthouse. The county courthouse, a weather-beaten old building, was also the home of the Concord town meeting, which met on the second Tuesday in March. Over the next ten years Franklin Pierce was a prominent figure in both the annual town meeting and the court sessions, including sessions held in other parts of the state.

THE GREATEST TRIAL LAWYER

Throughout the 1840s Pierce established a reputation as a brilliant trial lawyer. He had a special knack for understanding juries and appealed to them in a variety of ways, depending on the situation—sometimes using an intimate, friendly tone; other times relying on humor, ridicule, or sarcasm; and occasionally using drama. "In short," Nathaniel Hawthorne wrote, "he plays the part of a successful actor."

A New England Town Meeting

During the 1800s many cities throughout New England, including Concord, held regular town meetings. These gatherings gave the people in town a chance to talk about some of their concerns, ask questions of their leaders, and even vote on important city issues. Often they would discuss the city's budget and how to use it, as well as look at old and new laws. People commonly arrived early, so merchants took advantage of the moment to set up stands offering everything from gingerbread and candy to sweet cakes or a glass of ale.

Inside the courthouse people sat on wooden benches set up in long rows. Typically the first order of business was choosing who would be on the board of the meeting. In order to be fair to everyone, there was an effort to make sure most businesses were represented. Farmers, teachers, carpenters, clerks, accountants, blacksmiths, tanners, and constables were usually chosen.

In 1844 one of the issues that Concord dealt with at its town meeting was whether or not to continue to allow the sale of alcohol. A number of people present also wanted to make a decision on where the town stood on the issue of slavery.

Others also noted his remarkable abilities in the courtroom. A contemporary, the chief justice of New Hampshire, wrote, "The eloquence of Mr. Pierce is of a character not easily forgotten.

After Pierce's career as senator ended in 1842, he returned to his law practice.

He understands men, their passions and their feelings." And a few modern commentators have considered his record in relation to the state's court history and concluded that "Franklin Pierce was [probably] the greatest trial lawyer in New Hampshire history." He never seemed to run out of energy, passion, or enthusiasm.

As Pierce's reputation in the courtroom grew, he resisted the temptation to return to politics. Although he was invited by his colleagues to fill a Senate seat or run for governor, Pierce refused—much to the delight of his wife and his clients.

Just as Pierce's law career was soaring, he faced a sudden, unexpected tragedy. In November 1843 both of the Pierces' sons became seriously ill with typhus. Benny survived, but Frank died; he was four and a half years old.

Frank's death was devastating for the Pierces. Pierce spoke of his pain in a letter to his brother, Henry. "If you ever have a son, my dear brother," he wrote, "and are called to part with him you will be able to appreciate the depth of our sorrows, not till then."

Jane was particularly hard hit by the loss of her son. In a letter to a friend she said, "I hardly know how I go on from day to day without him." From that point forward, Jane was ill much of the time, and Pierce often made decisions that enabled him to remain close to her.

State and Local Politics

Although Pierce did not hold an elected position for ten years after resigning from the Senate in 1842, he became more active than ever in state and local political affairs. He was frequently at meetings of the Democratic Party, usually held in a Concord hotel. The **Whig Party** met in another hotel, and the contest between the two parties was spirited and frequently dirty. Each party used its own newspaper to attack the other. The Democrats' newspaper in Concord, *The Patriot*, was run by two young men who were studying law in Pierce's office.

Beginning in 1842 Pierce devoted much of his time to organizing the Democrats throughout the state. As chairman of the state party, he worked for unity on key issues, such as temperance, slavery, and the 1844 presidential election.

Pierce's efforts to give the Democrats control of Concord were complicated by the temperance issue. In the nationwide reform atmosphere of the 1830s and 1840s, many Americans came to feel that one of the best ways to improve society was to persuade people to sharply reduce their use of alcohol—or even to abstain completely. Most people in the **American Temperance Society** advocated very limited use of alcohol. Concord, like most of the nation, was sharply divided on the issue. Some were eager to ban the sale of alcohol as a basic first step, but

This American Temperance Society poster depicts a woman breaking a bottle-shaped cannon labeled "RUM."

others, especially the owners of taverns, were bitterly opposed to it.

Temperance was an idea that was close to Pierce's heart. He knew on a personal level what the consequences of drinking too much alcohol could be, as he had seen its effects on his own life. While he was a strong supporter of the temperance movement, since it mirrored his own struggles, he also was against the proposed statewide legislation to ban alcohol. As with other issues he felt that choosing whether or not to drink was up to the individual or the community instead of the government. It was a moral and religious choice—not a political one, he believed. This attitude created a problem for Pierce; when he was elected chairman of the state temperance society, he had to be very careful of what he said during meetings and speeches. If he promoted the idea of temperance too much, he would jeopardize his standing with the

Democratic Party. They felt he was not sticking to its principles of less government involvement. On the other hand, if he didn't speak out strongly enough about banning alcohol, the temperance societies would condemn him as a hypocrite. Trying to satisfy both sides was more than a little difficult.

In 1843, in an attempt at some kind of compromise, Pierce's committee created a petition that would effectively ban the sale of alcohol within Concord's limits. Almost two thousand men and women signed the petition. At the next voting no "wet" (antitemperance) selectmen were elected, and so Concord became what was known as a "dry" community—no alcohol was allowed in the city limits by law.

The issue of whether or not to ban alcohol throughout the United States would be debated for another seventy years, until the Eighteenth Amendment was passed in 1919, making the sale or distribution of alcohol within the country illegal. The amendment was repealed in 1933.

THE ELECTION OF 1844

In 1844, when James K. Polk was nominated for president by the Democratic National Convention, Pierce was working at his best to win the state for his friend. He used the campaign to heal the divisions within the party. In a letter to Polk he was enthusiastic about the Democrats replacing the Whigs as the party in power: "The party is thoroughly organized," he wrote, "and we are to have mass meetings in every county before the election." He predicted the Democrats would win the state by six thousand to ten thousand votes.

Pierce then went to work to help the party carry the state. He traveled from one end of the state to the other, giving

An 1844 campaign ribbon announces James K. Polk for president.

enthusiastic speeches day and night, finally returning home exhausted, his voice completely worn out. Polk won the election and carried New Hampshire by ten thousand votes, just as Pierce predicted. He rewarded Pierce by appointing him district attorney of New Hampshire. Two years later Polk offered him the cabinet post of attorney general, an offer that Pierce turned down. In a letter to the president Pierce explained that his wife's poor health forced him to decline the offer. "You know," he wrote, "that Mrs. Pierce's health, while at Washington, was very delicate. It is . . . even more so now."

THE SLAVERY ISSUE AGAIN

In May 1846 Americans learned that Mexican troops had fired on U.S. soldiers, apparently on American soil, and some had been killed. President Polk and Congress quickly issued a declaration of war. Many Americans had been eager for war with

President Polk requested for Congress to declare war on Mexico in 1846 after that country's troops fired on U.S. soldiers on American land.

Mexico for several years. For some it was part of the American idea of **Manifest Destiny**. The shooting incident on the U.S.-Mexico border gave President Polk a good excuse to ask Congress for a declaration of war.

Many people in New England were opposed to the war. They saw it as a plan by Southerners to add more territory for the expansion of slavery. This antiwar sentiment helped create troubling new splits in New Hampshire politics. In June a Whig was elected governor by the legislature. In addition, a new **Free Soil Party** had been formed, and one of Pierce's rivals among the Democrats, John P. Hale, was elected to the Senate.

Pierce was familiar with John Hale; their relationship dated all the way back to their time spent together as classmates at Bowdoin College. Even after they graduated, they continued to stay in touch, often writing to each other about various political matters. However, as the years passed, their opinions began to drift further and further apart until they were practically opposites on everything, especially the issue of slavery. It was enough to eventually destroy Hale and Pierce's personal and political friendship.

For the first time in almost twenty years the Democrats were not in full control of the state. Pierce had been warning that some kind of antislavery alliance was going to emerge and threaten the country's unity. (A decade later these opponents of spreading slavery would form the Republican Party.)

To help bolster the Democratic Party's ideals, Pierce and other party leaders in the state convention adopted a resolution explaining their position on slavery: "We deplore its [slavery's] existence, and regard it as a great moral and social evil," the document stated. "But . . . angry and external agitation, by exciting the prejudices of the slaveholding community, while it may endanger the Union, tends rather to fasten than to destroy the bonds of the enslaved."

The end of the resolution contained an idea that was going to have enormous consequences for the future of both Pierce and the nation: "Only the citizens of [the] States and Territories . . . can efficiently" end or alter slavery. This was to be the philosophy of **popular sovereignty** written into the Kansas-Nebraska Act in 1854.

The war with Mexico also kept New Hampshire divided, with the Whigs, like the Federalists in 1812, fiercely opposed to war. Consequently, Pierce's group produced one more resolution, urging all patriots to answer "the call to arms." Pierce himself was one of the first to answer that call, volunteering his services. Serving his country in war was part of his family's tradition, and he was eager for the chance to achieve military glory.

SEARCHING FOR GLORY

As soon as the United States declared war against Mexico, Pierce wanted to be a part of the battles. He was so eager to be involved that he was willing to serve as a private, but within a few weeks, the Polk administration appointed him colonel. He was ordered to help form an all-New England unit to be called the Ninth Regiment.

During the autumn of 1846, despite strong opposition to the war throughout New England, he gave stirring speeches urging young men to join the noble and patriotic cause. A newspaper that supported the war reported that an October speech was "one of the most able and eloquent speeches to which we have ever listened. The effect was truly electric."

Over the winter of 1846–1847 the size of the army was increased, and Pierce was promoted once again, this time to brigadier general. A few weeks later word came that an American force commanded by General Zachary Taylor was in trouble, and General Pierce was ordered to speed his preparations.

COMMANDING A REGIMENT

Throughout the spring of 1847 Pierce rushed to organize his regiment. It was an exciting time for him. For years he had dreamed of achieving the kind of military glory he had heard about throughout his boyhood. By the time he reached his forties, he thought the chance for military adventures had passed

Franklin Pierce served as a brigadier general during the Mexican War in 1847.

him by. Now, instead, he was being fitted for a handsome uniform. In addition, the ladies of the town presented him with an
elegant sword, and political associates gave him a fine horse.

Not surprisingly, Mrs. Pierce was dismayed at the thought of
her husband going off to war. Although she eventually accepted
it, she was filled with a sense of foreboding. To help ease her concern, Pierce arranged to have a woman stay with Jane. He had
his new law partner, Josiah Minot, look after his business affairs
and the practice.

Pierce and his aide, Major Trueman Ransom, somehow managed to have their 2,500 men, plus horses, weapons, and
equipment, on board the *Kepler* and ready to leave Portsmouth
Harbor by late May.

The voyage down the coast and across the Gulf of Mexico
was slow and difficult. Calm seas, no wind, and suffocating heat
made many of the soldiers ill. Pierce, on the other hand, felt won-
derful, full of vigor and passion for his new adventure. Day after
day he was down in the steamy cabins, bringing the men any
refreshments he could find or just talking to them with his infec-
tious enthusiasm. After the war many remembered these acts as
their commander's greatest heroism.

The *Kepler* finally landed at Vera Cruz late in June, and the
men marched inland to meet with the main army, under General
Winfield Scott. For three weeks General Pierce led his men inland
through 150 miles of enemy territory. The three-day journey to
bring wagons filled with essential supplies and weapons and
money was rough. Mexican snipers fired at the men, and they had
to fight off six attacks. A few of them were wounded, some were
felled by illness, and others were victims of the terrible heat, but
they finally caught up with the main army.

General Pierce and his troops land on the shores of Mexico. He led them 150 miles inland supplying troops with much needed supplies.

Now that Scott had the reinforcements he needed, he ordered the combined forces to march on Mexico City.

CONFUSION IN BATTLE

Pierce led his men into the Valley of Mexico, where they made their way over jagged rocks, remnants of an ancient volcano. As they advanced, Mexican skirmishers fired at them from the flanks, and artillery shells exploded around the Americans, splintering the rocks into deadly fragments.

Scott's army came up against a force of about seven thousand well-entrenched Mexicans. Pierce's recently recruited men had never been under artillery fire before, but fortunately the Mexicans' aim was a little too high, preventing many American casualties.

During the Battle of Contreras, Scott sent orders for Pierce's regiment to attack the left flank of the Mexicans. This was the moment Pierce had dreamed of. He leapt onto his horse and rode among his officers, encouraging them with stirring words.

His heart racing with excitement, Pierce rode to the front of the column. As the attack began, Pierce's horse was startled by the crash of an artillery shell. It slipped on the loose rocks and stumbled to the ground, crushing Pierce beneath it and severely injuring his knee.

Pierce was stunned by intense stabs of pain. As his orderly helped him to his feet, the pain in his groin and leg caused him to faint. As the orderly called for Major Ransom, an officer named Morgan, from another regiment, shouted, "Tell Ransom to take over! Pierce is a damned coward and has fainted!"

A number of men heard that statement, and it was repeated to others. A few days later, when Morgan learned the circumstances of Pierce's fall, he retracted his statement and apologized. But it was too late. The claim of cowardice lived on, and it would come back to haunt Pierce a few years later.

Pierce was soon mounted on the horse of a lieutenant who had been killed and made his way back to the front lines. The Battle of Contreras continued into the night, and Pierce stayed in the saddle through it all, spending several hours in drenching rain.

In the morning the Americans renewed the attack. Pierce, again on horseback, led a diversion to strike the rear of the enemy defense, forcing them into a wild retreat. The regiment continued to advance along a road strewn with dead and dying soldiers.

AMERICA'S MANIFEST DESTINY

In the 1840s a magazine editor named John L. O'Sullivan coined the term "manifest destiny" to describe the idea that it was America's clear (or manifest) destiny to expand its boundaries across the continent to the Pacific Coast. Throughout the decade and beyond the nation's presidents, with the support of Congress and the majority of the people, set to work to make this come to pass.

(continued)

First, in early 1845, Congress approved a resolution inviting Texas, which had won its independence from Mexico in 1836, to enter the Union as a state. Since Texas was a slave state, the push was made to annex the Oregon territory. After negotiations—and conflict with England that almost resulted in war—a treaty was signed. Oregon became a territory of the United States in 1848 and entered as a free state a decade later.

The War with Mexico was part of this drive to expand. The outgunned Mexicans put up a fierce resistance but were forced to surrender in 1847. In the Treaty of Guadalupe Hidalgo (1848) the United States gained a huge land area, including California, plus the sprawling region of today's Southwest—including New Mexico, Arizona, Utah, Nevada, and parts of Wyoming and Colorado. This was about half of Mexico's land.

In less than ten years the nation's boundaries had expanded to the Pacific—"from Sea to shining Sea." In 1853 President Pierce would complete U.S. acquisitions on the continent (except for the purchase of Alaska in 1867) by obtaining a strip of land on the border with Mexico.

Antonio López de Santa Anna, the Mexican commander, decided to make a stand at Churubusco and San Antonio, both well-fortified positions.

General Scott hoped to cut off Santa Anna from Mexico City, so he sent word for Pierce. When Pierce arrived, Colonel Noah E. Smith recalled, "He was exceedingly thin, worn down by the fatigue and pain of the day and night before, and evidently suffering severely. Still there was a glow in his eye, as the cannon boomed, that showed within him a spirit ready for the conflict."

General Scott, however, felt that Pierce was in no condition to lead his men into battle and ordered him to rest. Pierce was desperate. "For God's sake, General!" he exclaimed, "this is the last great battle and I must lead my brigade!"

VICTORY WITHOUT GLORY

Having persuaded General Scott to let him remain in command, Pierce eagerly led his men toward Mexico City. Santa Anna decided to make a last stand at Churubusco, just outside the city. The Americans had to wade across a water-filled ditch, forcing Pierce to leave his horse behind. He made it across the ditch on his injured knee, but as he and his troops neared the enemy, the pain and exhaustion proved to be too much, and he passed out.

Furious and embarrassed by his weakness,

Franklin Pierce proved to be a brave and enthusiastic leader during the Mexican War.

Pierce refused to let his men carry him to the rear. Instead he lay on the ground while the battle raged; bullets buzzing past him as the earth shook from exploding cannon shells. Without his leadership, Pierce's brigade did not do well. As the Mexican defenders fired from behind a wall, Pierce's men scattered, and many were killed or wounded.

Santa Anna asked for a truce after Churubusco, and the crippled Pierce was one of three commissioners to negotiate a peace treaty. The treaty was not well received by the troops, and it was during their grumbling that he learned about the earlier accusations of cowardice. Although Morgan had retracted his statement, the damage to Pierce's reputation remained.

In September the peace collapsed, and the fighting resumed. Pierce had gone to another general's headquarters to rest, trying to overcome exhaustion, pain, and a bout of stomach cramps. While he rested, the Americans stormed the castle of Chapultepec, Santa Anna's last stronghold. The Americans won but suffered heavy casualties, and Pierce's friend Major Ransom was killed. For the third time Pierce's men had fought a major battle, but the glory he so longed for still eluded him.

The way into Mexico City was now open, but it seemed likely that the Mexicans would resist one more time. Pierce and his orderly rushed to catch up to his troops. As soon as he arrived, he prepared for one last fight. It never happened. Instead, a white flag appeared, and the victors marched into Mexico City without opposition. The war was over.

General Pierce returned home in December 1847. While he had not achieved the kind of battlefield honors he had hoped for, he was a general who had served in a victorious army. In addition,

American troops stormed Chapultepec in September 1847, which led to the end of the Mexican War.

he had made many friends among the officers and was well liked and admired by his troops. Satisfied that he had proved himself in war, he was eager to return to civilian life.

THE UNLIKELY ELECTION CAMPAIGN *Seven*

$\mathcal{P}$ierce returned home to a hero's welcome. Large crowds cheered him, and the New Hampshire Legislature presented him with a handsome sword. The next five years were to be the most rewarding—and prosperous—of his life. They would include both his greatest personal triumph and his most devastating tragedy.

THE ZENITH

One of Pierce's biographers, in describing the years 1848 to 1852, wrote that "he reached his zenith!" He was at the peak of his profession, achieving greater wealth than he had ever dreamed possible, and he remained the head of his party in the state. So firm was his control of the New Hampshire Democrats that he became known as "the Dictator."

As a lawyer he was not considered a great scholar of law, but his enormous talents in the courtroom enabled him to master juries throughout New England. These talents were also great assets in his role as leader of the New Hampshire Democrats. His persuasive speaking style, for example, allowed him to heal rifts in the party. Even his unique ability to remember people, including their names, proved useful. In 1850, when a convention was held to revise the state constitution, it was not surprising that Pierce was the near-unanimous choice to chair it.

These few years were also the happiest for the Pierces as a family, although Jane was never easy for Pierce to get along with.

Her tuberculosis symptoms made her nervous and demanding. Although Pierce appeared to love his wife, she had great difficulty showing affection in return. She was delighted to have him at home and seemed genuinely happier than she had at any time in her life. In addition, the family had moved into a smaller rental house with another couple who managed daily affairs. This was very helpful for Jane, since she was often too ill even to prepare meals.

Above all else, it was their son Benny who made them happy. He was eight years old when his father returned from Mexico, and Pierce was thrilled to have him witness the town's welcome. He and Jane both adored the boy, and their hopes for the future were centered on him.

THE DARK HORSE

During the late 1840s the Democratic Party was struggling. In 1848 the Whigs had elected Zachary Taylor president. The Mexican war hero was a favorite with the people, and it looked like he would be elected to a second term. However, just after being part of ceremonies at the Washington Monument on July 4, he fell ill. A few days later the president was dead. Taylor was replaced by Millard Fillmore, a man most people did not know well. This change in leadership seemed to give the Democrats an unexpected chance to regain control of both the presidency and Congress.

In the spring of 1852 the country's Democratic leaders began searching for the strongest candidate to nominate for the November election. Lewis Cass, a former senator from Michigan who had been the losing Democratic candidate in 1848, seemed to be the front-runner. But there were other strong contenders: James

Buchanan of Pennsylvania, Stephen Douglas of Illinois, and William O. Butler of Kentucky.

Many party leaders felt it was not a strong field, so several of them traveled to New Hampshire to talk to Pierce about the possibility of trying for the nomination at the Baltimore convention, to be held in June. At first he was reluctant to consider it because he didn't think he had a chance. In letters to leading Democrats he stated his position: "My name must in no event be used [at the convention] until all efforts to harmonize upon one of the candidates . . . shall have failed. . . . If, however, there shall arrive a time [when a deadlock remains] you will of course . . . take such measures as the interests of the party and the country may demand."

Pierce left the door open, then, to becoming a **"dark horse"** candidate. That is, he would be a late compromise who might break a deadlock. It was a smart move. He knew that if he tried to have his name introduced early, the party's divisions would have overwhelmed his supporters. He was eager to run for the presidency, but he was not ready to.

At the start of the convention Cass was in a strong position, with 119 of the 192 votes needed for the nomination. But over the next two days the delegates conducted ballot after ballot without determining a winner. After about thirty ballots Cass began losing votes, while Douglas and Buchanan were gaining them. Late on Friday there was a sudden surge for Cass, and he climbed back to 123 votes by the end of the day. A little earlier, on the thirty-fifth ballot, the Virginia delegation introduced Pierce's name.

On the evening of the Democratic Party convention Pierce took Jane for a carriage ride rather than sit in a Boston hotel, waiting for a telegram, as others were doing. As Pierce drove the carriage through the bright spring greenery, he was met by his brother-in-law, Alpheus Packard. When Packard saw Pierce's wife, he "bowed low and elaborately, saluted her as the future 'Presidentress.'" The delegates in Baltimore conducted about ten ballots, with little movement. Then, on the forty-sixth ballot, Kentucky switched to Pierce, and three ballots later the North Carolina delegation started a landslide for Pierce.

Although Pierce and his wife had traveled back to Concord, waiting for the results of the vote there seemed harder, so soon they went back to Boston by train. A few days later, to distract them from the ticking clock, they took a carriage ride into the countryside. After a peaceful day they headed back into town only to be greeted on the road by Colonel Isaac Barnes on his horse. He brought news: Pierce had won! He was the Democratic candidate for president of the United States! Pierce could barely believe it, and Jane fainted.

Knowing that his wife would be unnerved by all of the attention, Pierce decided that she should go to Newport, Rhode Island, to rest and recover. While she was there, Benny wrote her a letter in which he made it clear that he was on his mother's side—he was not pleased about his father's nomination. "I hope he won't be elected," he wrote, "for I should not like to live at Washington and I know you would not either."

THE CAMPAIGN

William R. King, a senator from Alabama, was chosen as the vice presidential candidate, and the party platform was based on support for the Compromise of 1850. Pierce's Whig opponent

This photograph of Franklin Pierce was taken around the time of his candidacy for president of the United States.

was General Winfield Scott, the victorious general from the Mexican War.

Nathaniel Hawthorne, the great novelist and Pierce's friend since their days at Bowdoin, was asked to write the official campaign biography. Hawthorne was reluctant. He felt in the short space of eight or ten weeks, he could not do justice to the man and his career. He finally agreed, but in later years his reluctance was sometimes interpreted to mean that he did not think Pierce was a worthy subject for his talents. On the contrary, Hawthorne was one of Pierce's most loyal supporters.

While Hawthorne worked on the life story, pictures of the candidate were produced in enormous numbers. "His portrait is everywhere," Hawthorne wrote to a friend, "and in all sorts of styles—on wood, steel and copper, on horseback, on foot, in uniform, in civilian dress, in iron medallions, in little brass medals, and on handkerchiefs."

Pierce gave no speeches and did not travel in order to campaign, as was the custom of the time. He followed the advice not to write letters to state his position or to raise issues. He knew that Jackson had avoided taking a stand on controversial issues during his campaign, while Van Buren and Cass had hurt themselves by writing argumentative letters.

While the candidate was silent, his supporters were not. Because of his vigorous support of Andrew Jackson, who had been known as "Old Hickory," Pierce was sometimes called "Young Hickory." And since New Hampshire was famous for its granite hills and mountains, his campaign nickname became "Young Hickory of the Granite Hills." Throughout the country granite clubs were formed, and hickory poles were set up on village greens.

A campaign poster features Franklin Pierce (left) and his running mate William R. King.

Bands played and political officials who supported Pierce gave rousing speeches. Concord was especially crowded with well-wishers and those seeking jobs or favors, and a band frequently serenaded Pierce outside his home.

Just as most political campaigns contain some "mudslinging," so did Pierce's. Various newspapers began publishing insulting letters about the presidential candidate's war record and personal behavior. One letter labeled Pierce "the Hero of Many a well-fought Bottle," stating that he was an "immoral, dissipated man." Another stated that his "military service had been stained with cowardice." Pierce was frustrated and disappointed by such statements and confessed his feelings in personal letters to his friends. "Is it not sad that scoundrelism can obtain access to the columns of respectable papers?" he wrote. "That those whose very breath taints this air they breathe with falsehood can be received anywhere where a respect for truth is maintained. Above all," he continued, "is it not singular and singularly disgraceful that the Town of my residence should contain the chief fountains of malevolence, detraction and abuse poured out against me!" Over time he had no choice but to learn to ignore these stories and focus on proving them false through his campaign.

Pierce was learning how hard it was to make the transition from being a state and local political figure to becoming a national personality, vying for the highest office in the land. Outside of New England few people remembered him from his days in Congress, which had ended ten years earlier.

His uphill climb for recognition—and votes—was most likely much more difficult for him due to his family's lack of support. While they spent a pleasant summer along the coast, Pierce could not talk frankly with Jane about the pain caused by the personal attacks leveled at him or about how much he yearned to be elected president of the United States.

THE SURPRISING RESULT

The competition between Scott and Pierce was a tug of war. General Scott was a famous military hero but was also perceived by many as grouchy and pompous. Pierce was a general but had to continually fight off rumors of cowardice and alcoholism.

The one issue Pierce did face publicly—support for the Compromise of 1850—turned out to make a difference. The issue came up even before the nominations when a Richmond, Virginia, editor asked all the candidates to state their positions on the compromise.

Pierce was reluctant. He had worked hard to unify New Hampshire Democrats and was afraid a statement might splinter the party again, since opposition to the compromise remained strong. He finally agreed and, as his biographer said, "It proved to be the most important letter of his life." He believed strongly that the union of states had to be preserved at all costs. The compromise was the best way to hold the Union together, he argued, even though it required the North to accept the hated **Fugitive Slave Law**.

This bold stance actually helped to unify the Democrats as election day approached. Pierce's friends made whirlwind tours of eastern states, spreading pictures of him, his published statement on the Compromise of 1850, Hawthorne's biography, and a dozen shorter-length biographies. These efforts helped the Democrats win local elections in October in Pennsylvania, Ohio, and Indiana, raising hopes for November. In addition, just before Daniel Webster died in October, he told others that he supported Pierce for president.

On election day the united Democrats won handily, although the popular vote was close, with Pierce getting 1,601,274 to Scott's 1,386,580 votes. In the free states, Pierce was actually a minority candidate, losing by 14,000 votes. In the electoral vote, however, Pierce carried all but four states, 254 to 42. Scott won only Vermont, Massachusetts, Kentucky, and Tennessee.

Could Pierce maintain that party unity for four years? Would he be able to deal with the heavy opposition to him in

The Compromise of 1850

The matter of slavery had threatened the unity of the nation for decades. By 1820 the slave states of the South counted on having as many senators in Congress as the North, enabling them to block any Northern effort to ban slavery. In 1820, when Missouri applied for admission as a slave territory (a future state), Northerners were in an uproar. Henry Clay stepped in with a compromise—the Missouri Compromise (or Compromise of 1820)—that included the admission of Maine as a free state.

Clay's compromise kept the peace, but for how long? Former President Thomas Jefferson wrote to a friend, "This momentous question [the slavery issue], like a firebell in the night, awakened and filled me with terror. . . . This is a reprieve, but not a final sentence."

Thirty years later the issue flared up again when California applied for admission to the Union as a free state. This time the issue was more complex. There was no slave territory ready for admission as a state. But the huge area of the West acquired from Mexico was open to the question. Antislavery forces were determined to keep slavery out of the region. Southerners were just as insistent on spreading slavery to the region. They were willing to leave the Union if the expansion of slavery was prevented.

The aging Henry Clay once again offered a compromise that was finally accepted after months of debate. Both sides gave up something. The North was forced to swallow the bitter pill of the Fugitive Slave Law. In exchange, California was admitted as a free state. Utah and New Mexico became territories in which the question of slavery would be decided by the people (popular sovereignty).

the free states, where he would be a minority president? The morning after the election-day victory, Pierce rode to Hillsborough on a nostalgic journey to his boyhood haunts: the Pierce homestead, his old school, the places he had played as a boy. He may have been searching for some wellspring of strength to help him through the exciting but difficult four years ahead.

His good friend Hawthorne was not worried about the presidential term, however. "What luck that fellow has! . . . There are scores of men in the country that seem brighter than he is; but Frank has the directing mind, and will move them about like pawns on a chess-board, and turn all their abilities, to better purpose than they themselves could. . . . He is deep, deep, deep luck withal! Nothing can ruin him."

THE PRESIDENCY

The new year of 1853 brought crowds of well-wishers to the Pierce home, and there were frequent calls for informal speeches. Pierce faced it all calmly and with a growing sense of confidence. He was already thinking about his program: boosting the economy through increased overseas trade, keeping slavery off the national agenda, and adding more territory to the United States, as his predecessors had done.

As the family and a few servants began sorting clothes and personal items to serve the family for four years in Washington, even Mrs. Pierce and Benny were excited, and Mrs. Pierce seemed reconciled to fulfilling her role as First Lady.

THE TRAGEDY

January 6, 1853, dawned as a crisp, sun-filled morning. Almost as soon as the Pierces boarded the train to Concord, it pulled out of the station. Benny was entertaining his parents with stories of his escapades at school. Suddenly they were rocked by a violent jolt. The train lurched to the side, their car broke free, and it bounced down the embankment into a field. When Pierce searched through the chaos, he saw that Benny had been crushed in the wreckage and was dead. Quickly, he covered Benny's body with his cloak, but Jane had caught a glimpse of her mangled son and as one observer said, her "agony passes beyond any description." As for Pierce, he hid his grief for the moment, instead mustering the courage and strength the tragedy called for. "While deeply

Jane Pierce lost her youngest son Benny, pictured here, in a tragic train accident in 1853.

affected, [Pierce] showed all the self-possession and nerve which only characterizes great-hearted and noble men," stated a witness. "He gave all needful directions about the recovery of his little boy, still entangled in the wreck about him."

The days following the train accident were spent suffering long hours of grief and loss. Jane was often "frantic in her grief," according to her companion Abigail Kent Means. Pierce was gentle and kind to her as he struggled with his own emotions. A cousin stated, "There is but one opinion about him that he is one of the noblest and most tender hearted of human beings." Another biographer wrote, "It had been a terrible and shattering experience to those worshipping parents, to see their only boy mangled before their eyes, an experience from which neither of them ever recovered."

Benny's casket was carried by twelve of his schoolmates, and while Pierce accompanied his son's body for burial in Concord, Jane was not well enough to make the journey. Instead, she sought comfort in religion, yielding to her faith's belief that its savior was a stern God. Soon, she withdrew from all social events completely.

While biographer Roy Franklin Nichols has stated that Pierce never quite got over the loss of his son and that the tragedy negatively affected his abilities as president, other experts, such as Peter Wallner, firmly believe there is no evidence to support this belief whatsoever, as Pierce's actions and policies never changed.

Inauguration

On Inauguration Day a cold March wind and snow flurries swept through Washington and seemed to reflect the mood of the grieving president. He had hoped to have Benny share the moment with him, giving the boy a lifelong memory of his father's great triumph. Instead, Pierce faced the event alone, without his son or his wife by his side.

Pierce rode to the inauguration with outgoing President Fill-more. Cheering crowds boosted Pierce's spirits, and he stood up in the open carriage to wave. With his hand on a Bible, he **affirmed** the oath of office rather than following the tradition of

Franklin Pierce attended his inauguration in 1853 without his wife.

swearing it. The president-elect then stood to deliver his speech from memory as an oration, without notes, rather than as an address, with a written copy.

He spoke first of the great loss he was mourning: "It is a relief to feel that no heart but my own can know the personal regret and bitter sorrow over which I have been borne to a position so suitable for others rather than desirable for myself." Later he said, "You have summoned me in my weakness; you must sustain me by your strength."

Pierce was famous for his public speaking and didn't disappoint the people on this blustery day. As he warmed to the elegant phrases he had memorized, the crowd cheered him on, with shouts of "He's really got it goin' now."

He spoke of the need, above all, of preserving the union of states: "I am moved by no other impulse than a most earnest desire for the perpetuation of that Union which has made us what we are. . . . Let it be impressed upon all hearts that, beautiful as our fabric is, no earthly power or wisdom could ever reunite its broken fragments."

In speaking of slavery, he made it clear that "involuntary servitude . . . is recognized by the Constitution. I believe that it stands like any other admitted right, and that the States where it exists are entitled to efficient remedies to enforce the constitutional provisions. I hold that the [compromise measures] of 1850 are strictly constitutional and to be unhesitatingly carried into effect." He believed that, by adhering to the compromise, the slavery question "is at rest, and that no sectional or ambitious or fanatical excitement may again threaten the durability of our institutions or obscure the light of our prosperity."

He also outlined other basic goals of his presidency. In domestic policy he hoped to expand trade and to encourage westward movement. And in foreign policy he did not want to shy away from acquiring territory. "My Administration," he declared, "will not be controlled by any timid forebodings of evil from expansion."

The rest of the day was spent shaking hands with the scores of people who crowded the White House. The throng was larger than expected, primarily because there was to be no Inaugural Ball, due to the president's period of mourning. Many came as well-wishers, but others were job seekers hoping for political appointments. The Pierce administration had begun. He was the nation's youngest president until the twentieth century.

DIFFICULT BEGINNINGS

President Pierce needed some good news—something positive to help him climb out of the somber mood of the previous two months and to restore the self-confidence he had always relied on. Instead, he found himself facing more bad news.

First, the gloomy mood was accentuated a few weeks after the inauguration when Mrs. Fillmore, the wife of the outgoing president, died suddenly in the Willard Hotel. More bad news arrived days later. William Rufus King, Pierce's vice president, had been an important choice because of his previous alliance with James Buchanan, one of Pierce's rivals for the nomination. But King was already in the last stages of tuberculosis. After the election he went to Cuba in the hope of finding a cure. He was given permission to take the oath of office there. King returned home to his Alabama plantation on April 18, but died the next day.

He had not served a single day as vice president. Pierce decided not to choose another vice president and became the only president in U.S. history to serve his entire term without one. David R. Atchison, president pro tempore of the Senate, was next in the line of succession.

Pierce also faced unpleasant problems with Mrs. Pierce. Since the White House was being remodeled and was not ready for the First Lady to move in, she was staying with friends in Baltimore. Although Pierce was eager

Vice President William King passed away before he could ever serve in that capacity. Pierce is the only president in U.S. history to serve without a vice president.

to see his wife again and share his inaugural address with her, she was not interested in hearing it. Frustrated and preoccupied with his upcoming inauguration, Pierce decided to return to Washington the next morning. Jane had planned to give her husband a lock of Benny's hair that she had saved, hoping he would wear it during the ceremonies, but when the time came, she was too upset to do so. The two found it almost impossible to communicate how they were feeling, which drove them apart.

A Subdued First Lady

Jane Pierce never fully recovered from Benny's death—especially the gruesome image of seeing his body so badly mangled. For the next two years she remained a recluse. She did eventually move into the White House, along with Abigail Kent Means, her dear friend and aunt. Mrs. Means provided companionship and also served as hostess for public functions.

For the first year after Benny's death Jane did not attend public functions not only because she was grieving but because staying at home and remaining quiet was part of the era's mourning ritual. Although she was not seen often, she did attend church each Sunday and was present each night for dinner, whether it was a simple dinner

The Quest for Harmony

President Pierce knew that he faced enormous obstacles. The Democrats had pulled together well enough to elect him president and to win control of both houses of Congress, but that did not mean the party was united—far from it. Old divisions remained, both personal and regional. The men who had competed with Pierce for the nomination still had strong support in Congress. In addition, the Democrats always relied on gaining votes from both the North, where many were opposed to slavery, and the South, where most continued to support their constitutional right to own slaves.

with her husband or an elaborate meal with visiting political or personal friends. In April 1853 she even accompanied Nathaniel Hawthorne on a boat ride on the Potomac.

By 1855 Jane began appearing in public more often, and several women had very positive impressions of her. Mrs. Robert E. Lee, wife of the greatest and most popular Confederate general in the Civil War, wrote in a letter to a friend, "I have known many of the ladies of the White House, none more truly excellent than the afflicted wife of President Pierce. Her health was a bar to any great effort on her part to meet the expectations of the public in her high position, but she was a refined, extremely religious, and well-educated lady." Another friend admired her "gentle but powerful influence [which] was deeply and constantly felt, through wise counsels and delicate suggestions, the purest, finest tastes, and a devoted life."

The country itself was becoming increasingly divided over the slavery issue. The Compromise of 1850 had held the union of states together, but Northerners were upset over the Fugitive Slave Law. This law led more and more of them to join the abolitionists' crusade. Northerners were also worried that Southern leaders were searching for ways to expand slavery into the new territories acquired from Mexico.

Pierce's primary goal during his presidency was to create harmony within the party and to preserve the Union. Selecting a cabinet was challenging, and every choice seemed to invite criticism from one direction or another. William L. Marcy, of New York, became secretary of state, for example, but he had also tried to win the presidential nomination. Many people felt that Pierce had too many Southerners among his seven cabinet members. Jefferson Davis (Mississippi) was secretary of war, James C. Dobbin (North Carolina) was his choice for the navy, and James Guthrie (Kentucky) was his choice for the treasury. These choices won support for the president in the South, but later, many critics said the choices showed that he favored the expansion of slavery.

Another cabinet member—James Campbell of Pennsylvania, as postmaster general—stirred a different kind of controversy. Campbell became the first Catholic to be a member of any administration, and his appointment came at a time when a powerful anti-immigration sentiment was sweeping the country. People who called themselves "nativist Americans" had even formed the Nativist, or **Know-Nothing Party**, which showed surprising strength in the elections of the 1850s.

The Pierce cabinet, when finally approved by the Senate, managed to represent the diversity within the party, and that was a credit to Pierce's skill with people. He was so successful that his was the only cabinet in history that had no changes in personnel throughout an entire presidential term. Even more important, his cabinet never had a single hint of scandal or corruption—unlike many others.

In spite of this success, however, Pierce soon had to pay a price for maintaining harmony within the party. And, in paying that price, he made decisions that would cost him dearly. The judgment that he was a poor president and that his administration was a failure grew out of his choices involving slavery and the Kansas-Nebraska Act.

THE KANSAS-NEBRASKA ACT

In January 1854 Illinois senator Stephen A. Douglas introduced the Kansas-Nebraska Bill. The bill had several purposes: to create the territories of Kansas and Nebraska, to open new lands for settlers, to repeal the Missouri Compromise of 1820, and to let the new territories decide for themselves whether they'd allow slavery. Making Kansas and Nebraska territories would allow the government to make treaties with the American Indians living in the region. This would allow settlers access to more land. Repealing the Missouri Compromise would allow new territories to decide the slavery question, an idea that intrigued Southern voters.

President Pierce did not like the bill. He did not want the issue of slavery to come up during his administration, and he knew that the passage of this measure would touch off a storm of controversy. But support for the bill was strong—too strong for Pierce to fight. Douglas had proposed the plan because the land to be annexed provided a perfect route for a railroad that cut across the continent from Chicago. Many senators in states east of Illinois were eager to have the railroad go through their states. A railroad that traveled along a northern route through the Western frontier would provide countless opportunities for investors to buy land along the routes—land that could then be resold to settlers.

A number of senators made it clear that they would block Pierce's appointments and other measures if he failed to support the Douglas bill. He gave in, and after furious debate in Congress, the Kansas-Nebraska Act was passed, and the president signed it into law.

The impact was both immediate and far-reaching. While Nebraska was thought to be too far north to support slavery, proslavery and antislavery forces poured into Kansas. Each side wanted to be in the majority in order to control the writing of the state Constitution. The side that won could actually gain control of the Senate for its side. So much was at stake that violence erupted,

Proslavery soldiers with artillery were ready to battle for control of Kansas in 1855 to 1856.

and a small-scale civil war raged in Kansas in 1855 and 1856. This period of unrest is called **Bleeding Kansas**.

The repeal of the Missouri Compromise of 1820 resulted in a deep split in the Democratic Party. The Southern wing of the party sided with the proslavery settlers, who established a capital at Lecompton, Kansas. Democrats who opposed slavery supported the antislavery forces, who were established at Topeka. The slavery issue, which Pierce had been so anxious to avoid, was now beginning to tear the country apart. The Democrats remained divided through the rest of the decade and, in 1861, the Southern wing of the party joined other proslavery groups in voting for secession. Pierce's secretary of war, Jefferson Davis, became president of the rebel government, which was called the Confederate States of America.

Pierce desperately wanted to save the nation from a civil war. He believed so strongly in the Union and the Constitution that he would do anything in his power to preserve it. He declared the northern, or Topeka, government to be treasonable and ordered it to disband. He sent troops to Kansas to enforce his decision and finally succeeded in restoring order.

The president continued to believe that the abolitionists were a small fringe group, led by a few wild-eyed fanatics. Throughout his term he continued to rely on the army to try to establish order, insisting that any effort to interfere with slavery would be unconstitutional and could lead only to war.

FOREIGN POLICY

Pierce hoped that developing an aggressive foreign policy would help to defuse the slavery time bomb. He was motivated in part

by the success of his immediate predecessors in the White House. Polk had become a national hero, for example, by acquiring nearly all of Mexico's land north of the Rio Grande. Although Pierce pursued an aggressive policy, he had very little success in gaining new land.

The only expansion of territory he accomplished was the Gadsden Purchase—a strip of land along the Mexican border. Secretary of War Jefferson Davis had urged the purchase because it provided an excellent southern route for a transcontinental railroad. Pierce had offered $50 million for a large area of northern Mexico. Instead, for $10 million, the United States acquired about 45,000 square miles of land in what is now southern Arizona and New Mexico.

Pierce also made several attempts to acquire Cuba. He soon learned, however, that every such move touched off a storm of protest by antislavery forces, who claimed that the president was the tool of Southern states, which wanted to expand slavery any way they could.

A crisis developed when Pierce tried to "detach" Cuba from Spain. The president ordered his ministers in European countries to come up with a plan. In the autumn of 1854 the ministers to Britain, France, and Spain met in Ostend, Belgium. The U.S. minister to France, Pierre Soulé, was an avid supporter of slavery. Their plan, which included a threat of using force to take Cuba should Spain be unwilling to sell the island, was leaked to newspapers in a somewhat garbled form. The document, called the **Ostend Manifesto**, infuriated Northerners, because they saw it as a certain sign of Pierce working with the slave states.

The Final Two Years

By 1855 Pierce was on the defensive. The sporadic warfare in Bleeding Kansas continued to foreshadow the nation's drift toward civil war. The Whig Party was falling apart and soon ceased to exist. In the midterm elections Democrats lost control of Congress. The Know-Nothings gained strength, and so did a new party, the Republicans. The Republican Party had been formed by men, including the little-known Abraham Lincoln, who were opposed to any extension of slavery into the territories.

The last two years of Pierce's term were dominated by efforts to ease the crisis in Kansas. In his final State of the Union message, delivered on December 2, 1856, he blamed the anti-slavery forces for pushing the nation toward civil war. Any change "in the relative condition of the white and black races in the slaveholding States . . . is beyond their legal authority," the president said. "It [change] cannot be effected by any peaceful instrumentality of theirs. . . . The only path to its accomplishment is through burning cities, and ravaged fields, and slaughtered populations."

Pierce did enjoy a few modest successes. He gained some popularity in the North and West by favoring grants of land to the railroads pushing westward. He encouraged trade by establishing treaties with several countries and gained fishing rights off the coast of Canada. The most far reaching treaty was one with Japan, negotiated by Commodore Matthew C. Perry. Japan agreed to diplomatic and trade relations, ending its long-term isolation from the West.

In addition, Pierce took a firm stand against Great Britain on two occasions. First, when the British considered expanding their colonial holdings in Central America, he objected, saying they were violating earlier treaties with the United States. The British dropped their plans. Later, during the Crimean War, Pierce dismissed the British minister to Washington, charging him with recruiting troops on U.S. soil. The British government was furious, and for a few weeks the two countries were close to war, but the crisis passed without further trouble.

THE BITTER LAST YEARS

In the spring of 1856 Pierce felt confident that the Democratic Party would nominate him for a second term, but a series of events clouded the issue. The most serious problem was the continuing civil war in Kansas. The country's drift toward disunion was also illustrated by an incident that took place in the Senate. In late May 1856 a Southern senator, Preston Brooks, entered the Senate Chamber and used his cane to beat the Northern senator Charles Sumner almost to death. Fearing more violence, Northern senators began carrying weapons.

Pierce blamed agitators on both sides for the situation in Kansas, but more and more Northerners were saying that the president had failed to establish order in the territory. Anger at Pierce increased in June, just before the Democrats met in Cincinnati to nominate their candidate for the 1856 election.

When the Democrats met, Pierce knew he would have competition, especially from James Buchanan, but he felt certain of receiving at least 145 votes on the first ballot. Instead, he learned that Buchanan received 135.5 votes and that he only got 122.5.

A political cartoon depicts southern senator Preston Brooks beating northern senator Charles Sumner on the senate floor in 1856.

Buchanan went on to win the nomination and the election. Four years later the Republican Abraham Lincoln was elected, and the Union was torn apart by the Civil War.

Pierce was terribly disappointed in not being nominated but also realized that his party needed someone who could unite the opposing factions. In his desire to keep the slavery issue off the nation's agenda, Pierce had come up against a no-win situation. He backed the Kansas-Nebraska Act, which some saw as a serious mistake. However, he really had little alternative. If the bill had not passed, Manifest Destiny would have come to a screeching halt. Settlers would not have traveled west of the Missouri River, and the transcontinental railroad would have remained only a dream.

When westward expansion ran into the issue of slavery, there was no simple solution. Choosing the nation's expansion over the abolition of slavery was the decision that Pierce finally made—and it was an understandable one. Later, Pierce's decision to expand U.S. territory through purchasing Cuba only led people to believe that he was a pawn of slave interests—a perspective that was not true.

Resigned to his loss, Pierce headed back to New Hampshire. Mrs. Pierce was so ill that she had to be carried from the White House. After she recovered, the Pierces made two long trips abroad before finally settling down in Concord.

In 1860 Jefferson Davis and several others urged Pierce to try again for the presidential nomination. However, Pierce continued to blame the North for dividing the country. And, after the Civil War began in April 1861, he insisted the North was wrong to resort to force. He also stirred up hostility by saying that Lincoln's Emancipation Proclamation was unconstitutional.

Mrs. Pierce died in 1863, and Pierce had few friends in his remaining years. When Lincoln was assassinated, a mob marched to Pierce's home and threatened him. A few friends did stay close to him, including Nathaniel Hawthorne, who wrote that Pierce should have been praised, not condemned, for his inability "to admit any ideas that were not entertained by the fathers of the Constitution and the Republic."

Franklin Pierce sat for this photograph around the time of losing the nomination for president of the United States.

During the summer of 1869 Pierce suffered from a severe stomach ailment. He died during the night of October 8, 1869. His body lay in state in the New Hampshire capitol, and he was buried in Concord. Fifty years passed before the state erected a statue in his honor.

ASSESSMENTS OF PRESIDENT PIERCE

Some Americans dismiss Pierce as a weak and ineffective president. In opinion polls he is usually ranked at the very bottom of the list, generally in the company of James Buchanan and Warren G. Harding. Many critics have been harsh in their assessments of him. For example, a contemporary politician, Gideon Welles, wrote in 1868 that Pierce was "a vain, showy, and pliant man . . . [who] by his errors and weakness broke down his administration, and his party throughout the country."

Later critics were just as blunt. Theodore Roosevelt said, "[Pierce was] a small politician, of low capacity and mean surroundings, proud to act as the servile tool of men worse than himself, but also stronger and abler. He was ever ready to do any work the slavery leaders set him."

President Harry S. Truman agreed. "Pierce was the best looking president the White House ever had—but as president he ranks with Buchanan and Calvin Coolidge."

Few modern writers offered more positive assessments until the recent work of Peter A. Wallner, who has written one of the two scholarly biographies of Pierce that have appeared in the past eighty years. Wallner, library director of the New Hampshire Historical Society, believes that scholars have tended to focus on Lincoln and the Civil War, overlooking Pierce's courageous efforts to avoid the conflict. In his epilogue to the second volume of his biography, Wallner wrote:

> In the divisive political climate of the 1850s, Pierce's consistent legal and ethical conduct kept the nation on a course of prosperity and growth. Slavery was not a problem that could be solved within the antebellum [pre-war] political system. The Pierce administration's honest, efficient, legalistic, nationalistic stewardship was the best the nation could have hoped for at the time.
>
> His inflexibility was both a weakness and a strength. . . . He sacrificed his own reputation and career in a failed bid to preserve the Union.

Many historians view President Franklin Pierce as a weak and ineffective leader. However, some see him as a president who fought to keep the nation on a steady path during that time in American history.

1804
Born November 23, Hillsborough, New Hampshire

1824
Graduates Bowdoin College

1827
Admitted to New Hampshire bar

1828
Elected to New Hampshire legislature

1832
Elected to U.S. Congress

1834
Marries Jane Means Appleton, Amherst, New Hampshire

1800

1835
Elected to Congress second time

1837
Elected to U.S. Senate

1846
Serves in Mexican War as brigadier general

1852
Nominated for presidency; wins election in November

1856
Democratic Convention fails to nominate him for a second term

1869
Dies October 8

1870

NOTES

CHAPTER 1

p. 9, "one of the most charming, charismatic, and interesting men": Peter A. Wallner, quoted in Koziol, John, "Author Takes Fresh Look at Pierce," *The Citizen*. http://www.citizen.com/apps/pbcs.d1l/article/AID=/20071028/CITIZEN (accessed 11/13/2007).

p. 9, "deep, deep, deep . . .": Nathaniel Hawthorne, quoted in Nichols, Roy Franklin, *Franklin Pierce: Young Hickory of the Granite Hills*. Philadelphia: University of Pennsylvania Press, 1931, 1968, p. 217.

p. 10, "robust, active, and devilish": Franklin Pierce, quoted in Wasserman, Benny. *Presidents Were Teenagers, Too*. Victoria, B.C., Canada: Trafford Publishing, 2007, p. 44.

p. 10, "She was a most affectionate . . . ": Franklin Pierce, quoted in Nichols, p. 10.

p. 17, "He conquered me by his faith . . . ": Zenas Caldwell, quoted in Nichols, p. 26.

CHAPTER 2

p. 21, "his innate self-confidence . . .": Hawthorne, Nathaniel. *Life of Franklin Pierce*. Honolulu, Hawaii, 2002 (reprinted from 1900 edition), p. 21.

p. 21, "made themselves practiced in oratory . . .": Quoted in Nichols, p. 28.

p. 22, "his native habit . . . ": Hawthorne, p. 23.

p. 23, "Frank Pierce is the most popular man . . .": Quoted in Hawthorne, p. 61.

p. 23, "The eloquence of Mr. Pierce . . .": Quoted in Nichols p. 47.

p. 24, "The Democratic party was to become . . .": Nichols, p. 47.

p. 27, "at home in political [meeting] and tavern . . .": Nichols, p. 92.

CHAPTER 3

p. 30, "I consider slavery . . .": Franklin Pierce, quoted in Wallner, Peter. *Franklin Pierce: New Hampshire's Favorite Son*. Concord, NH: Plaidswede Publishing, 2004, p. 72.

p. 31, "One thing must be perfectly apparent . . .": Franklin Pierce, quoted in Wallner, *Franklin Pierce*, p. 67.

p. 35, "the greatest frolic of my life.": Clement March, quoted in Wallner, *Martyr for the Union*. Concord, NH: Plaidswede Publishing, 2007, p. 316.

p. 36, "The interests of the country . . .": Andrew Jackson, quoted in Hawthorne, p. 28.

CHAPTER 4

p. 40, "So long as I feel . . .": Franklin Pierce, quoted in Wallner, *Franklin Pierce*, p. 57.

p. 41, "Liberty and Union . . .": Daniel Webster, quoted in King, David C. *The United States and Its People*. Menlo Park, CA: Addison-Wesley Publishing Co., 1996, p. 229.

p. 41, "snap the cords which bind . . .": John C. Callhoun, quoted in King, p. 291.

p. 43, "his usual elasticity of spirits . . .": Franklin Pierce, quoted in Nichols, p. 104.

p. 43, "Oh, how I wish . . .": Jane Pierce, quoted in Nichols, p. 104.

CHAPTER 5

p. 44, "In short . . . he plays the part . . .": Hawthorne, p. 54.

p. 45, "The eloquence of Mr. Pierce . . .": quoted in Hawthorne, p. 61.

p. 46, "Franklin Pierce was [probably] the greatest . . ." : Quoted in Koziol, John. "Author Takes a Fresh Look at Franklin Pierce" *Boston Globe*, Oct. 28, 2007.

p. 46, "If you ever have a son . . .": Franklin Pierce, quoted in Wallner, p. 105.

p. 47, "I hardly know how I go . . .": Jane Pierce, quoted in Wallner, p. 105.

p. 49, "The party is thoroughly organized . . .": Franklin Pierce, quoted in Nichols, p. 132.

p. 50, "You know that Mrs. Pierce's health . . .": Franklin Pierce, quoted in Hawthorne, p. 64.

p. 52, "We deplore its [slavery's] existence . . .": Quoted in Nichols, p. 139.

p. 53, "Only the citizens . . .": Quoted in Nichols, p. 139.

CHAPTER 6

p. 54, "One of the most able . . .": Quoted in Nichols, p. 140.

p. 58, "Tell Ransom to take over!": Quoted in Nichols, p. 161.

p. 60, "He was exceedingly thin . . .": Colonel Noah E. Smith, quoted in Hawthorne, p. 77.

p. 61, "For God's sake, General!": Franklin Pierce, quoted in Hawthorne, p. 78.

CHAPTER 7

p. 64, "He reached his zenith!": Quoted in Nichols, p. 171.

p. 66, "My name must in no event . . .": Franklin Pierce, quoted in Nichols, p. 200.

p. 67, "he bowed low and elaborately . . .": Alpheus Packard, quoted in Wallner, *Franklin Pierce*, p. 202.

p. 67, "I hope he won't be elected . . .": Benny Pierce, quoted in Wallner, *Franklin Pierce*, p. 202.

★ ★ ★ ★ ★ ★ ★ ★ ★ ★ ★ ★ ★ ★ ★ ★ ★

p. 69, "His portrait is everywhere . . .": Nathaniel Hawthorne, quoted in Nichols, p. 209.

p. 70, "the Hero of Many . . .": Quoted in Wallner, Franklin Pierce, p. 206.

p. 70, "his military service has been stained . . .": Quoted in Nichols, p. 205.

p. 71, "Is it not said . . .": Franklin Pierce, quoted in Wallner, *Franklin Pierce*, p. 206.

p. 72, "It proved to be . . .": Quoted in Nichols, p. 205.

p. 73, "This momentous question . . .": Thomas Jefferson, quoted in Nichols, p. 201.

p. 74, "What luck that fellow has . . .": Quoted in Hawthorne, p. 217.

Chapter 8

p. 75, "her agony passes beyond . . .": Quoted in Wallner, *Franklin Pierce*, p. 242.

p. 75, "While deeply affected . . ." : Quoted in Wallner, *Franklin Pierce*, p. 242.

p. 77, "There is but one opinion . . .": Quoted in Wallner, *Franklin Pierce*, p. 242.

p. 78, "It had been a terrible . . .": Nichols, p. 225.

p. 79, "It is a relief to feel . . .": Franklin Pierce, quoted in Miller Center of Public Affairs, *Franklin Pierce Speeches*, http://www.millercenter.virginia.edu/scripps.digital archive/speeches/spe_1853_0304_pierce (accessed 7/20/2007).

p. 79, "I am moved by no other impulse . . .": Franklin Pierce, quoted in Miller Center.

p. 79, "involuntary servitude . . . is recognized . . .": Franklin Pierce, quoted in Miller Center.

p. 79, "the slavery question 'is at rest . . .'" : Franklin Pierce, quoted in Miller Center.

p. 80, "'My Administration,' he declared . . .": Franklin Pierce, quoted in Miller Center.

p. 83, "I have known many of the ladies . . .": Mrs. Robert E. Lee, quoted in The White House website, *Biography of Jane Pierce*. http://www.whitehouse.gov/history/firstladies/jp.14.html (accessed 8/5/2007).

p. 83, "her gentle but powerful influence . . .": Quoted in Olive Tardiff, "Jane Appleton Pierce," http://www.hampton.lib.nh.us/hamptonbiog/janepierce.htm (accessed 8/5/2007).

p. 90, "Any change in the relative condition . . .": Franklin Pierce, quoted in Whitney, Robin Vaughn. *The American Presidents*. Pleasantville, NY: The Readers Digest Association, 1996, p. 116.

p. 93, "his inability to admit any ideas . . .": Nathaniel Hawthorne, quoted in Nichols, p. 217.

p. 95, "a vain, showy, and pliant man . . .": Gideon Willes, quoted in Nichols, p. 533.

p. 95, "[Pierce was] a small politician . . .": Theodore Roosevelt, quoted in Kenin, Richard and Justin Wintle, eds. *Dictionary of Biographical Quotations*. New York: Knopf, 1978, p. 600.

p. 95, "Pierce was the best looking . .": Harry S. Truman, quoted in DeGregorio, William A., *The Complete Book of U.S. Presidents*. New York: Barnes & Noble, 1984, 2002, p. 207.

p. 96, "In the divisive political climate . . .": Peter A. Wallner, quoted in Kozio.

GLOSSARY

abolition the act of abolishing slavery

affirm to make a promise to uphold the nation's laws without making a religious statement

American Temperance Society an organization formed in 1826 by people who took a pledge to never drink any alcoholic beverages

annex to take or to attach a territory

"Bleeding Kansas" term for the fighting between proslavery and antislavery forces in the Kansas Territory

Compromise of 1850 a series of measures that enabled California to enter the Union as a free state in exchange for creating the Fugitive Slave Law, which enables slave owners to recover escaped slaves

"dark horse" a surprise candidate usually offered as a compromise in a dead-locked contest

Free Soil Party a political party that was active in the 1848 and 1852 elections

free state a state in which slavery was not allowed

Fugitive Slave Law a federal law designed to enforce the return of runaway slaves

gag rule a rarely used congressional rule that prevents the discussion or even the introduction of a particular topic

Know Nothing Party anti-immigration political party from the 1850s

Manifest Destiny the idea that Americans had the clear (or manifest) destiny to expand westward across the continent to the Pacific Ocean

Missouri Compromise an agreement between the proslavery and antislavery factions regarding the western territories

Ostend Manifesto a report by U.S. envoys in Europe suggesting ways of acquiring Cuba; when the document was leaked to the press, Pierce's critics said it was proof that he was planning to expand slaveholding territories.

popular sovereignty the practice of allowing the voters of a territory or state to decide whether or not to permit slavery

temperance the movement to reduce alcohol consumption to very modest amounts or to ban it altogether

utopia an ideal society in which participants shared everything, based on their needs; most utopias failed within a few years

Whig Party a political party, active from the 1830s to the 1850s, that supported a strong federal government

FURTHER INFORMATION

BOOKS

Evensen Lazo, Caroline. *Franklin Pierce*. Minneapolis, MN: Twenty-First Century Books. 2007.

Ferry, Steven. *Franklin Pierce*. Chanhassen, MN: Child's World. 2009.

Venezia, Mike. *Franklin Pierce: Fourteenth President 1853–1857*. Danbury, CT: Children's Press, 2005.

Zamora, Dulce. *How to Draw the Life and Times of Franklin Pierce*. New York: PowerKids Press, 2006.

WEB SITES

Franklin Pierce at the Internet Public Library

www.ipl.org/div/potus/fpierce.html

Visit this site for a brief biography of Franklin Pierce.

Franklin Pierce at the White House

www.whitehouse.gov/history/presidents/fp14.html

Fast facts about President Franklin Pierce are available at this site.

The Pierce Manse

www.piercemanse.org

This site is dedicated to New Hampshire's only president and his home.

BIBLIOGRAPHY

Hawthorne, Nathaniel. *Life of Franklin Pierce*. Honolulu, Hawaii: University Press of the Pacific, 2002 (reprinted from the 1900 edition).

Kenin, Richard and Justine Wintle, eds. *Dictionary of Biographical Quotations*, New York: Knopf, 1978.

Koziol, John. "Author Takes a Fresh Look at Franklin Pierce," *Boston Globe*, Oct. 28, 2007.

Nichols, Roy Franklin. *Franklin Pierce: Young Hickory of the Granite Hills*. Philadelphia: University of Pennsylvania Press, 1931, 1969.

Tardiff, Olive. *They Paved the Way: A History of New Hampshire Women*. Bowie, MD: Heritage Books, Inc., 1980.

Wallner, Peter. Vol. I *Franklin Pierce: New Hampshire's Favorite Son* and Vol. II *Franklin Pierce: Martyr for the Union*. Concord, NH: Plaidswede Publishing, 2004, 2007.

Whitney, Robin Vaughn. *The American Presidents*. Pleasantville, NY: The Readers Digest Association, 1996.

INDEX

Pages in **boldface** are illustrations.

★ ★

ABOUT THE AUTHOR

David C. King is a full-time freelance writer. He has written more than seventy books for children and young adults, primarily on American history. He has written numerous books for Marshall Cavendish Benchmark.

He and his wife, Sharon, live in the Berkshires at the junction of New York, Connecticut, and Massachusetts—a great jumping-off point for their research and travels.